IMAGES
of America

ILLINOIS MILITARY MONUMENTS

ON THE COVER: In 1869, a monument was erected in the center of Franklin Square to commemorate McLean County citizens who died in the Civil War. The inscription read, "McLean County's Honored Sons: Fallen—but not Forgotten" with engravings of the names of the 700 soldiers who died in service. The structure featured four statues of soldiers—infantry, cavalry, zouave, and marine—and a life-size figure of a colonel atop an 18-foot shaft. Over the years, the monument began to disintegrate. A committee was created to fix it, but unfortunately, its material was so fragile that the names were nearly obliterated and the entire monument was in danger of collapsing. Former governor Joseph Fifer lobbied for the city to tear down the monument and build a new one in Miller Park in Bloomington (part of this monument is currently still standing). The lower half of the monument was saved and is currently in the Bloomington neighborhood of Briarwood. (Courtesy of the Detroit Photographic Company.)

IMAGES
of America

ILLINOIS MILITARY MONUMENTS

Maj. Lorenzo A. Fiorentino (Ret.)

ARCADIA
PUBLISHING

ISBN 978-1-4671-0319-0

Published by Arcadia Publishing
Charleston, South Carolina

Printed in the United States of America

Library of Congress Control Number: 2018965121

For all general information, please contact Arcadia Publishing:
Telephone 843-853-2070
Fax 843-853-0044
E-mail sales@arcadiapublishing.com
For customer service and orders:
Toll-Free 1-888-313-2665

Visit us on the Internet at www.arcadiapublishing.com

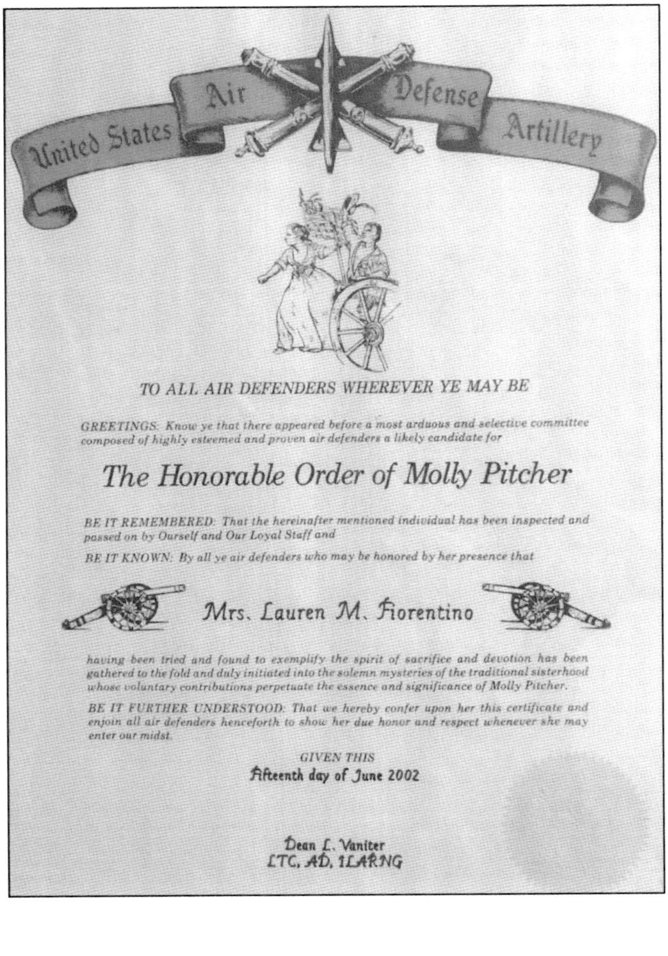

United States Air Defense Artillery

TO ALL AIR DEFENDERS WHEREVER YE MAY BE

GREETINGS: Know ye that there appeared before a most arduous and selective committee composed of highly esteemed and proven air defenders a likely candidate for

The Honorable Order of Molly Pitcher

BE IT REMEMBERED: That the hereinafter mentioned individual has been inspected and passed on by Ourself and Our Loyal Staff and

BE IT KNOWN: By all ye air defenders who may be honored by her presence that

Mrs. Lauren M. Fiorentino

having been tried and found to exemplify the spirit of sacrifice and devotion has been gathered to the fold and duly initiated into the solemn mysteries of the traditional sisterhood whose voluntary contributions perpetuate the essence and significance of Molly Pitcher.

BE IT FURTHER UNDERSTOOD: That we hereby confer upon her this certificate and enjoin all air defenders henceforth to show her due honor and respect whenever she may enter our midst.

GIVEN THIS
Fifteenth day of June 2002

Dean L. Vaniter
LTC, AD, ILARNG

This book is dedicated to my wife, Lauren, and our two adult children. Thank you for always supporting me in everything that I choose to attempt. The journey is as important as the destination.

CONTENTS

ACKNOWLEDGMENTS

Thank you to my family and friends who encouraged me to complete this book. Special thanks to everyone who contributed photographs: Sgt. David Davies, James Collinet, Daniel DuVerney, Michael A. Holub, Ken Knack, Melissa LaCoy, Ramona Machay, Adriana Schroeder, Bill Waters, Mark Werner, Department of Veterans Affairs, National Cemetery Administration, Hines Media Service, Illinois Military Museum, Illinois National Guard, International Film Service in Chicago, Detroit Photographic Company, and the National Register of Historic Places.

All images are from the author's collection unless otherwise noted.

My hope is that the creation and publishing of this work, in itself, is a memorial to all of the brave women and men from the great state of Illinois who have served our nation in wartime and in peacetime.

Introduction

Illinoisans and the Illinois National Guard have served the state and nation for nearly 300 years. Under the French, Kaskaskia residents participated in the first militia muster on May 9, 1723. From 1778 to 1779, the Illinois militia joined Col. George Rodgers Clark and fought the British, contributing to the victories of the American Revolution.

Illinois citizen-soldiers first federalized in 1809, when militiamen constructed stockades, or blockhouses, to defend themselves and their families against British and hostile Indian attack during the War of 1812. Capt. Abraham Lincoln enlisted during the Black Hawk War, becoming a member of the Illinois National Guard on April 21, 1832. At the Mexican Battle of Cerro Gordo in April 1847, soldiers of the 4th Illinois Volunteer Infantry Regiment nearly captured Mexican general Santa Anna. His captured wooden leg resides in the Illinois State Military Museum at Camp Lincoln and draws visitors from around the world. When the Civil War broke out in 1861, Illinois volunteers answered Pres. Abraham Lincoln's call, providing 259,100 men. Illinois gave the third largest in numbers after New York and Ohio and suffered around 35,000 casualties. Three current units have lineages that date to the Civil War.

On April 26, 1898, the governor activated eight Illinois National Guard regiments to serve in the Spanish-American War for two years or the duration of the war. Illinois troops were sent overseas to fight a war sparked by the sinking of the USS *Maine* in Havana harbor, Cuba. Carl Sandburg, poet and Abraham Lincoln biographer, enlisted as a private in the Illinois National Guard out of a sense of patriotism. Elements of the Illinois Militia fought in the Mexican Border War in 1917.

From 1917 to 1919, World War I took soldiers from the prairies of Illinois to the battlefields of France. The 8th Illinois Infantry, one of the first all-black units, fought under the French. World War I brought the National Guard into the modern age of warfare. In the autumn of 1918, more than one million Americans fighting in France engaged in the bloodiest battle in the history of the US military. Over 47 days of warfare, nearly 100,000 US doughboys were wounded, and more than 26,000 were killed in action in a chapter of the Great War that few Americans today truly understand. The Illinois 33rd Golden Cross Division played an important role in helping bring World War I to an end. The 33rd attained the distinction as the only American division to fight while organized with both French and British forces as well as fighting under its own flag. Illinois gave 351,153 men to the Army and Navy of the United States during the war. By the end of the war, more than 5,000 men from Illinois had given their lives. In 1918, Col. Otis Duncan became the highest-ranking African American soldier in the entire American Expeditionary Force during World War I.

During World War II, Illinois sent 987,000 men and women to Europe and the Pacific; 22,000 gave their lives. In the Pacific, they liberated towns from the Japanese. In 1942, a total of 325 men from Company B, 192nd Tank BN, from Maywood, suffered severe hardship as POWs at the hands of the Japanese during the Bataan Death March. In Europe, the 106th Cavalry received many accolades for the rescue of a Belgian king from the German Nazis.

Established in 1927 and becoming its own branch on January 1, 1956, the Illinois Air National Guard provided support during the Korean War. Soldiers on the Army side functioned as replacements and trainers. During the Vietnam War, 3,009 Illinois residents were killed or went missing in action. The Illinois Army and Air National Guard provided logistics support. One unit, the 126 Service and Support Company, from Quincy, deployed as a complete unit.

At home, the National Guard was called upon to supplement state and local authorities in maintaining civil control in the cities and on college campuses. In the 1980s and 1990s, the focus turned to transformation and training to meet the expanded role of providing support to humanitarian operations, including six NATO missions. Since the fall of the Soviet Union, the Illinois National Guard has become a partner in safeguarding the people of other nations. Specifically, Illinois partnered with Poland; this partnership proved valuable during the Global War on Terrorism. When Iraq invaded Kuwait in 1990 during the Gulf War, the Illinois National Guard was part of the coalition that liberated the country and provided follow-up protection in Operation Southern Watch. Through peacekeeping operations in Macedonia and Bosnia, Ukraine, and the establishment of a partnership for peace with Poland, Illinois has shown that it is a good neighbor to the world.

Following the terrorist attacks of September 11, 2001, the Illinois National Guard has taken on a major role in supporting the Global War on Terrorism in Afghanistan, Iraq, at home, and wherever freedom and liberty are threatened. It has responded to several national emergencies. It has deployed more than 11,500 Illinois soldiers and 10,000 Illinois airmen in support of operations Iraqi Freedom, New Dawn, Enduring Freedom, and Inherent Resolve since 2001. Thirty-four Illinois National Guard soldiers have fallen during operations in Iraq and Afghanistan. In 2011, the 126th Air Refueling Wing deployed to support the no-fly zone over Libya.

The Illinois National Guard has been a major contributor to every major conflict in our nation's history, and has provided a ready and relevant force to respond to any accident or incident that should arise, state or federal. The memorials on these pages are a testament to all service members but especially to those who made the ultimate sacrifice in service to the United States of America.

One

The Indian Wars

Black Hawk was born around 1767 in the village of Saukenuk; he grew up very anti-American and supported the British during the War of 1812. Commonly referred to as a chief, he held no official position in his tribe. He did possess natural leadership skills that inspired many warriors to follow him. After the Black Hawk War, he toured the eastern United States and dictated his autobiography. He died in Iowa in 1838.

This statue of Abraham Lincoln depicts him as a captain in the Illinois Militia. It was unveiled on September 24, 1930, by the State of Illinois in Dixon, Lee County, on the north shore of the Rock River. The brass plaque has the inscription: "Was stationed here during the Black Hawk War in 1832, as captain of volunteers. On April 21, 1832, he enlisted at Richland Creek, Sangamon County, and was elected captain. He was mustered into state service at Beardstown on April 22 and into United States service at the mouth of Rock River May 3. At the mouth of Fox River on May 27, he was mustered out and on the same day re-enlisted as a private in Captain Elijah Iles' Company. At the expiration of this enlistment, he re-enlisted on June 16, at Fort Wilbourn in Captain Jacob M. Early's Company, and was finally mustered out of service on July 10, 1832, at White Water River, Wisconsin."

The actual sculpture used for the Lincoln Memorial in Dixon is titled *Lincoln at 23*, or *Young Captain Lincoln* and was sculpted by Leonard Crunelle. It was cast by the American Bronze Company and dedicated in April 1930. It is a full-length, bronze sculpture of Lincoln standing on a granite base and depicted as a captain during the Black Hawk War in Illinois in 1832. Lincoln holds a sword in his left hand and has a coat over his right arm.

Apple River Fort, located in present-day Elizabeth, was built in less than a week and was one of many frontier forts hastily completed by settlers in northern Illinois and southern Wisconsin following the onset of the 1832 Black Hawk War. It was one of the few forts attacked during the war and the only one attacked by a band led by Black Hawk himself. The Battle of Apple River Fort lasted about an hour and ended with Black Hawk's forces withdrawing. The fort suffered one militia man killed in action and another wounded. After the war, the fort stood until 1847, occupied by squatters before being sold to a private property owner who dismantled the building. (Courtesy of Sgt. David Davies.)

In 1996, a replica of the fort was built by a nonprofit organization next to the site of the original Apple River Fort. The replica was based on earlier archaeological investigations of the site, which revealed information about the layout and settlement at the fort. The earliest settlers in the vicinity of the Apple River Fort, probably miners, likely arrived more than a decade before the fort's construction. The miners settled the site and built log cabins around its current location and obtained fresh water from a nearby spring. In 2001, the State of Illinois took over operations of the site and designated it the Apple River Fort State Historic Site. (Courtesy of Sgt. David Davies.)

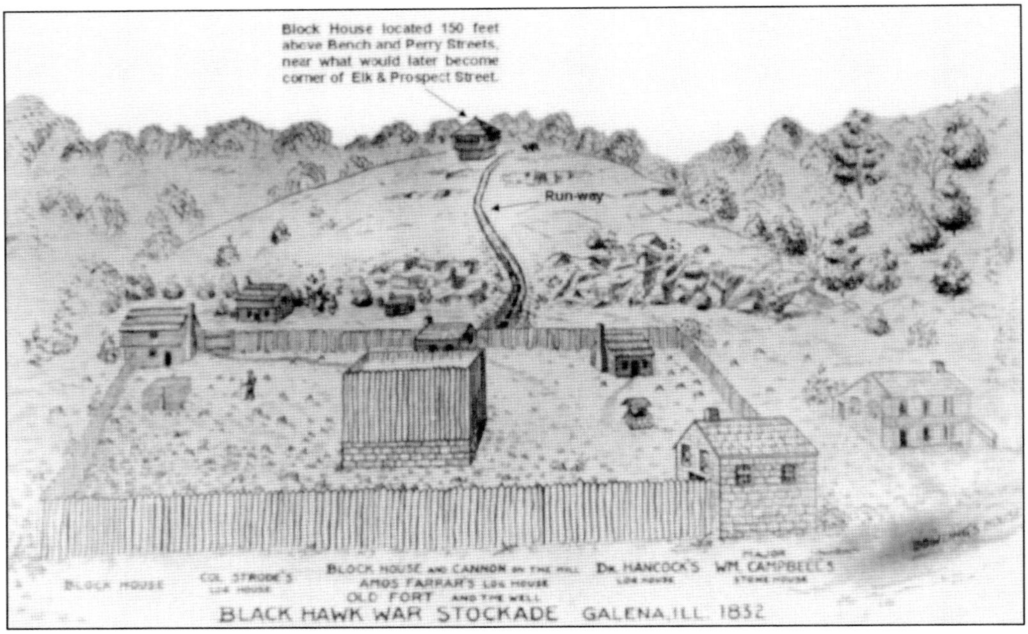

The drawing above depicts the layout of the Galena stockade, which was a typical layout of the time. The Black Hawk War of 1832 created the need to prepare for an Indian attack. The people of Galena constructed a stockade. Within the fort were homes to be used as a refuge for the settlers of the Galena area. After the war, the old stockade became a museum. The photograph below shows the 1920 dedication of Stockade Monument in Galena by the Daughters of the American Revolution.

The Black Hawk War Monument is located near Kent on the site of Kellogg's Grove, an early settlement established in 1827 on a mail route between Peoria and Galena and now listed in the National Register of Historic Places. It honors those killed in the Black Hawk War, including the final Illinois battle, which occurred at this grove in June 1832. Abraham Lincoln, a member of the Illinois Militia, helped to bury five of the slain men. The remaining soldiers were originally buried throughout the area at the spots where they fell. Fifty years after the war, local farmers collected the remains and buried them in one enclosure on top of this hill overlooking the Yellow Creek Valley. The 34-foot-high monument was dedicated in 1886. (Courtesy of Sgt. David Davies.)

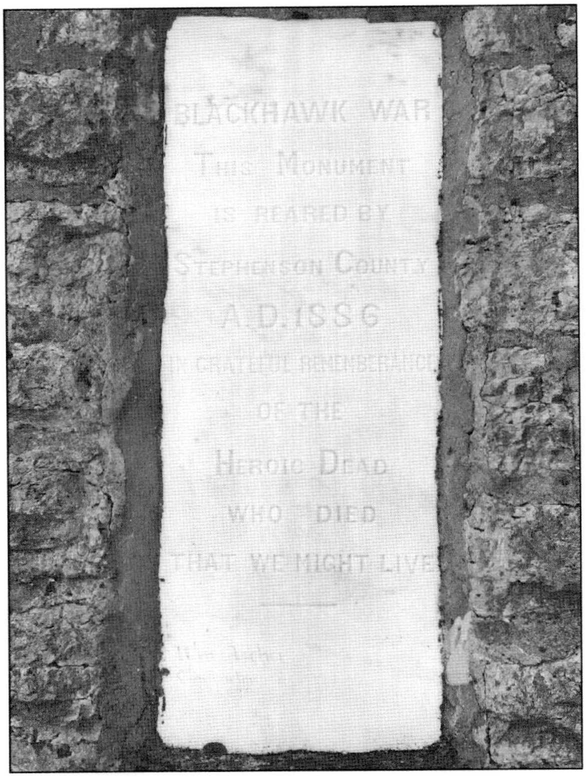

In these photographs, marble slabs that are inserted in the stone Black Hawk War Monument in Kellogg's Grove can be seen. The white marble slabs read, "Battle field of Kelloggs Grove, where was fought June 25, 1832 the decisive battle between the forces of the United States and the great Indian Chief Blackhawk. US Forces commanded by Col. John Dement," "Blackhawk War, This monument is reared by Stephenson County A.D. 1886 in grateful remembrance of the heroic dead who died so that we might live," and "Killed on the field of battle 23. Names as far as Known, Benjamin Scott, drummer boy, Ames Private, S Howard, Sublette, Wm Hale, J. Fowler, Crawford, A. Bond, Hallett, W. Allen, J. Black, A. Bradford, I. Meek, Savery, Floid, W.B. Manenson, M. Lovel, B. McDade Corporal, Aaron Halley, P. St. Vrain, Indian Agent." (Both, courtesy of Sgt. David Davies.)

The dedication ceremony in September 1914 drew a large crowd to Chandler Park. The Macomb monument honors and pays tribute to two War of 1812 heroes in particular—Gen. Alexander Macomb and Commodore Thomas Macdonough, for whom the city and county are named. Macomb and Macdonough led the nation to victory in crucial battles at Plattsburgh and on Lake Champlain on September 11, 1814.

The restored War of 1812 monument in Chandler Park was rededicated on May 8, 2016. The monument now has a concrete patio, landscaping, and a concrete sidewalk leading to it. After the war, the federal government encouraged development of western Illinois by creating the Military Tract for veterans of the War of 1812. The land was surveyed in 1816–1817 before most counties were developed, and 2.8 million of those acres were distributed to former soldiers.

The *Black Hawk* statue, also known as *The Eternal Indian*, is a sculpture by Lorado Taft located in Lowden State Park near Oregon, Illinois. The statue looks over the Rock River on a 77-foot bluff overlooking the city. Taft began creating this statue in 1908, and it was dedicated in 1911. He noted at the dedication that the statue seemed to have grown out of the ground, which was once home to the Eagle's Nest Art Colony, which Taft founded in 1898. The statue was planned by Taft and several of his students and associates at the art colony, which is now part of the Taft Campus of Northern Illinois University and is adjacent to Lowden State Park. The citizens of Oregon and the vicinity, with help from the Department of Natural Resources, purchased the former Eagles' Nest land so that it could be turned into a memorial park. In 1945, the 63rd General Assembly designated the 273-acre site as Lowden State Park. On November 5, 2009, the *Black Hawk* statue was listed in the National Register of Historic Places.

The *Black Hawk* statue stands 125 feet above the Rock River, though its height only accounts for 48 feet of that. *Black Hawk* weighs in at 536,770 pounds and is said to be the second-largest concrete monolithic statue in the world. The statue has a long blanket, and stares across the river with folded arms. Reinforced with iron rods, the hollow statue is eight inches to three feet thick. The interior is accessible to park employees through a door at the base. The outer surface, composed of cement, pink granite chips, and screenings, is three inches thick. Though not publicized at the time of construction, original funds were exhausted before the completion of the work, and future Illinois governor Frank Lowden stepped in to ensure that the statue was completed and erected. Shortly after Governor Lowden died, the legislature appropriated $25,000 toward the cost of a memorial to him.

This *Black Hawk* statue stands at the entrance of the Black Hawk State Historic Site and was created by David Richards. The Black Hawk State Historic Site, in Rock Island, occupies the historic site of the village of Saukenuk, the home of Native Americans of the Sauk Nation. The park is on a 150-foot bluff overlooking the Rock River. It is most famous for being the birthplace of the Sauk warrior Black Hawk. The Sauk developed military and economic ties with British Canada. Due to these ties, the Sauk expected British military assistance. The disputed 1804 St. Louis Treaty between Quashquame and William Henry Harrison led to the transfer of Illinois lands to the US government, including Saukenuk. The Sauk did not consider this treaty valid, and continued to live at the village. The disputed cession of this area to the US government was the catalyst for the Black Hawk War. Black Hawk led the Sauk and Fox Indians in many battles from the War of 1812 to the Black Hawk War of 1832.

The Stillman Valley Blackhawk War Memorial is located on the site of the first battle of the Blackhawk War, which occurred on May 14, 1832. Twelve soldiers who died during the battle are buried here. The memorial was dedicated on May 11, 1901, by the Memorial Association of Stillman Valley. Stillman Valley was founded in 1876. A creek running through the community was named after Major Stillman of the Illinois Militia, who led troops in the first battle of the Black Hawk War. The battle and the creek became known as Stillman's Run. The day after the battle, Abraham Lincoln helped bury the dead soldiers. One side of the monument lists the names of the honored fallen volunteers. The memorial to this battle reads, in part, "Here, on May 14, 1832, the first engagement of the Black Hawk War took place, when 275 Illinois militiamen under Maj. Isaiah Stillman were put on the run by Black Hawk and his warriors."

In 1901, the Battlefield Memorial Association of Stillman Valley erected a monument with funds from the 42nd Illinois General Assembly. One side of the memorial reads, "The Illinois volunteers who fell at Stillman's Run, May 14, 1832, in an engagement with Black Hawk and his warriors." In 1934, the State of Illinois erected a battlefield monument on the site, seen at left. (Both, courtesy of James Collinet.)

Two

The Civil War

"A house divided against itself, cannot stand. I believe this government cannot endure, permanently, half slave and half free. I do not expect the Union to be dissolved—I do not expect the house to fall—but I do expect it will cease to be divided. It will become all one thing or all the other. Either the opponents of slavery will arrest the further spread of it, and place it where the public mind shall rest in the belief that it is in the course of ultimate extinction; or its advocates will push it forward, till it shall become lawful in all the States, old as well as new—North as well as South," stated Abraham Lincoln on June 16, 1858. This sculpture by John McClarey, "Out of Court," representing Lincoln and client Melissa Goings, was dedicated in Metamora on August 22, 2009.

In 1869, a 49-foot-high monument, with a Lemont limestone base, was erected in the center of Franklin Square to commemorate the 700 McLean County citizens who died in the Civil War. An inscription reads, "McLean County's Honored Sons: Fallen—but not Forgotten." The structure featured four statues of soldiers (infantry, cavalry, zouave, and marine) and a life-size figure of a colonel atop an 18-foot shaft.

This photograph, taken in 1895, shows a veteran and a young girl standing by a cannon that is part of the McLean County Civil War memorial. The monument was built by the Haldeman Marble Works Company of Bloomington, Illinois, at a cost of $15,000.

The Bureau County Soldiers and Sailors Monument is located in Princeton, Illinois, and is the focal point of Courthouse Square. The monument was dedicated by the citizens of Bureau County on January 1, 1913, to honor the county's Civil War veterans. It cost $25,000. It is made of granite and bronze and features plaques on the sides, which list the men from Bureau County who participated in the Civil War. It stands 50 feet high and is topped by a winged Victory statue.

In June 1861, Gov. Richard Yates appointed Ulysses S. Grant colonel of the rebellious 21st Illinois Volunteer Regiment. Grant soon taught the unruly men military discipline and led them against pro-Confederate guerrillas in Missouri. Because of his demonstrated leadership ability, Grant was then made brigadier general in command of the volunteer district at Cairo. On February 14, 1861, Confederate brigadier general Simon B. Buckner, an old friend of Grant's, yielded to Grant's hard conditions of "no terms except unconditional and immediate surrender." Buckner's surrender of 14,000 men made Grant a national figure almost overnight, and he was nicknamed "Unconditional Surrender" Grant. This victory also won him promotion to major general of volunteers. This memorial was erected in 1886 by the surviving veterans of the 21st Regiment Illinois Volunteer Infantry to commemorate the site where Grant received his commission as a general in 1861.

The 71st Regiment Illinois Volunteer Infantry organized at Camp Douglas in Chicago and served in the Union army during the Civil War. The regimental commander was Col. Othniel Gilbert. It was mustered into Federal service on July 26, 1862, for a term of three months and was mustered out of service in Chicago on October 29, 1862. The regiment moved the next day to Cairo. It served in various garrisons in southern Illinois and western Kentucky. Company K, led by Capt. James Creed, was responsible for protecting two bridges along the Big Muddy River and the Illinois Central Railroad in southern Illinois from Confederate sympathizers. The regiment remained in Cairo for 10 days, then was ordered to Columbus, Kentucky. Two companies were detached from the regiment and stationed at Mound City. Colonel Gilbert, with three companies, was ordered to Moscow, Kentucky, and Lieutenant Colonel Burnsides, with three companies, was ordered to Little Obion Bridge to guard bridges and railroad tracks. The regiment suffered 23 casualties, all enlisted men who died of disease.

The Carroll County Civil War Soldiers and Sailors Monument is located on the Carroll County courthouse grounds in Mount Carroll. On October 24, 1884, Carroll County Civil War veterans organized the Soldiers and Sailors Reunion Society of Carroll County. It was decided that the society would build a monument to honor the 1,284 Civil War veterans of the county. The society members suggested that the monument, which was made of Barre granite, be placed on the courthouse square in Mount Carroll. The county board voted to contribute $6,000 for the project, and the City of Mount Carroll provided $400 to construct the cement steps and background. It was unveiled and dedicated in Mount Carroll on October 6, 1891, before a crowd of more than 5,000 people. A band from Savanna led a parade of marchers, including members of various Grand Army of the Republic posts, the Knights of Pythias, the Select Knights of America, and schoolchildren.

Pictured is the cavalryman statue at the base of the monument. The monument consists of a 50-foot vertical shaft with a Lorado Taft sculpted soldier holding a flag at the top. Lewis H. Sprecher of Lanark posed for the statue and made several trips to Taft's Chicago studio to model for it. On the shaft of the monument are eight engraved symbols representing the various Army groups that the men of Carroll County fought in during the Civil War. Most of the men fought under Generals Grant, Sherman, McPherson, or Logan. They fought in Alabama, South Carolina, Mississippi, Georgia, or Tennessee. The monument also includes the names of the 12 battles that the men of Carroll County fought in—Atlanta, Chickamauga, Corinth, Fort Donelson, Gettysburg, Hatchie's Bridge, Nashville, Resaca, Shiloh, Stones River, Vicksburg, and the Wilderness.

Pictured is the infantryman statue at the base of the monument. Between the two soldier sculptures it reads, "Carroll County: To The Memory Of The Men Who Saved The Union That Their Example May Speak To Coming Generations." The short phrases "Slavery Abolished" "Peace Restored" and "Courage—Endurance" flank the monument on the other three sides. Two large cannons are positioned on either side of the monument, and a pyramid of cannon balls rests on the ground near the rear of the monument. An annex was added later when county officials determined that there were many names missing from the original honor roll list.

The 41st Illinois Volunteer Infantry is pictured here in Memphis, Tennessee, in 1863. From left to right are (seated) Col. Isaac Campbell Pugh; (standing) Adj. William C.B. Gillespie, Lt. Isaac Mc Bean (103rd Illinois), and Q.M. Isaac Rinaldo Pugh. The 41st Illinois Volunteer Infantry was organized at Decatur in July 1861 by Col. Isaac C. Pugh. It was mustered into service on August 5 and was assigned to the command of General Prentiss. On September 8, the infantry moved with other troops, under General Grant, to Paducah, Kentucky, and assisted in fortifying that city. The 41st engaged in numerous battles and skirmishes. On July 12, 1863, at the Battle of Jackson near Vicksburg, Mississippi, the 41st, under command of Colonel Pugh, lost more than two thirds of the men who went into the engagement, including many line and field officers. Also, the regimental flag of the 41st was captured. On January 4, 1865, the 41st Illinois Volunteer Infantry was consolidated with the 43rd Illinois Infantry by order of Gen. O.O. Howard, forming companies H and G. (Courtesy of Meg Terreson.)

The 31st Illinois Volunteer Infantry Regiment from Little Egypt (which was the bottom 16 counties of southern Illinois) greatly contributed to the Union effort in the Civil War. Put into service on September 18, 1861, under Col. John Logan, the regiment went on to become one of the greatest in the Union. It consisted of about 1,100 men from the 18 southernmost counties of Illinois. The regiment marched a combined 4,000 miles in the western theater with Generals Grant and Sherman. The 31st Illinois fought 14 battles and 25 skirmishes, including the battles of Donelson, Shiloh, and Vicksburg, and was present at the Confederate surrender of the Army of Tennessee in North Carolina. The regiment lost 471 men of the original 1,100, a death count topped by no other Illinois regiment.

The Olio Township Cemetery Civil War Veterans Memorial in Eureka was dedicated on May 30, 1868, to the 29 Woodford County men of the 86th Illinois Infantry who were killed in action. The inscription on the monument reads, "A Tribute To The Memory Of Our Comrades, The Fallen Heroes of Co. A. 86. Ills. Vol. Infantry. The 86th Regiment was mustered into service at Peoria, Illinois on August 27, 1862 and discharged at Washington City June 6 1865." Two sides of the monument list the names, ranks, and location where each soldier was killed. Another side lists the battles that the regiment fought in: Perryville, Chickamauga, Lookout Valley, Buzzard Roost, Resaca, Rome, Dallas, Big Shady, Kennesaw Mountain, Chattahoochee, Peach Tree Creek, Atlanta, Jonesboro, Ebenezer Church, Savannah, Averysborough, and Bentonville.

The *Mother Bickerdyke* monument is located outside of the Knox County Courthouse in Galesburg. It was dedicated on May 22, 1906, by the Grand Army of the Republic Galesburg Post 45, the Women's Relief Corps, and the Village of Galesburg. The bronze and granite monument depicts a wounded soldier receiving the tender ministrations of a nurse on a Civil War battlefield. The nurse is Mary Ann Ball Bickerdyke. The soldier represents the thousands of men to whom Bickerdyke gave comfort during the Civil War. Mary Ann Bickerdyke, also known as Mother Bickerdyke, was a hospital administrator for Union soldiers. During the war, she became chief of nursing under the command of Gen. Ulysses S. Grant and served at the Battle of Vicksburg. By the end of the war, with the help of the US Sanitary Commission, Mother Bickerdyke had built 300 hospitals and aided the wounded on 19 battlefields, including the Battle of Shiloh and Sherman's March to the Sea. The illustration below, *Our Women and the War* by Winslow Homer, honors Civil War nurses and was featured in *Harper's Weekly* on September 6, 1862.

The Kankakee Civil War Memorial is located on the Court Street side of the Kankakee Courthouse and was dedicated on August 2, 1887. The memorial consists of a life-size bronze statue of a Union army soldier standing atop an eight-foot granite pedestal inscribed, "In Memory of the soldiers of Kankakee County who fought for the Union. 1861–1865. Love of Country is a Nation's strongest safeguard." The memorial was a project of the local Whipple Post of the Grand Army of the Republic. The veterans' group conducted a two-year public fund drive that raised more than $6,000. In 1897, the Whipple Post obtained two large coastal defense guns, also known as Parrott rifles, used during the Civil War and mounted east and west of the memorial. During World War II, they were hauled away and melted down during a scrap metal drive.

In 1909, a 58-foot-tall granite obelisk was dedicated to the Confederate dead buried at the North Alton Confederate Cemetery in Alton. Over time, the cemetery fell into disrepair, and the grave identifications were lost. The obelisk marks the final resting place for thousands of Confederate soldiers who died in captivity at the Union prison at Alton; there are no individually marked graves for these men. In 1862, the first transfer of prisoners included 1,640 soldiers. Shortly after the prisoners' arrival, there were reports of smallpox outbreaks. The Confederate prisoners were buried individually with wooden stakes to mark their graves. The rusticated granite obelisk stands atop a stepped base and a concrete plinth. Tablets fixed to each side of the plinth list the names of 1,354 Confederate soldiers who died in the Alton prison. (Courtesy of the Department of Veterans Affairs, National Cemetery Administration, History Program.)

The 36th Illinois Regiment Volunteer Infantry, also known as the Fox River Regiment, served in the Union army during the Civil War. The 36th Illinois Regiment recruited soldiers exclusively from the Fox River Valley area; eventually, 1,200 local young men responded to the call. The 36th Illinois Regiment was organized at Camp Hammond in Montgomery, just south of Aurora, by Col. N. Greusel. The regiment was mustered in by Colonel Brackett on September 23, 1861, for three years of Federal service. The men covered over 10,000 miles while serving under four different commanders. They took part in 10 major battles as well as countless minor engagements and skirmishes. The regiment was mustered out on October 8, 1865. It had 11 officers and 193 enlisted men who were killed in action or who died of their wounds and 1 officer and 127 enlisted men who died of disease, for a total of 332 fatalities.

The Civil War Soldiers Monument stands at Lakeside Cemetery in Pekin, Tazewell County. The monument was dedicated in May 30, 1905. The inscription reads, "In memory of our soldiers of Pekin, Ill." It was commissioned and erected by the Woman's Relief Corps No. 236. The original Grand Army of the Republic Hall was located on Court Street in Pekin. The notable area commander, Col. Charles Turner, served during the Civil War as the commander of the 108th Illinois Volunteer Infantry. He was brevetted brigadier general, US Volunteers, on March 26, 1865, for "faithful and meritorious services during the campaign against the city of Mobile and its defenses."

The Peoria Soldiers and Sailors Monument was dedicated on October 6, 1899. Pres. William McKinley and Frederick Triebel were at the dedication. Triebel was a native of Peoria and sculpted the work in Italy over a six-year period. The marble base and shaft were quarried in Maine, and the bronze figures were cast in Pistoia, Italy, in 1898. The monument is 68 feet tall. The Ladies' Memorial Day Association decided a monument should be built in honor of Civil War dead. They raised $40,000 from various picnic fundraisers, children's penny drives, the Peoria County Board of Supervisors, the City of Peoria, and the Martin Kingman plow company.

Triebel named his sculpture *Defense of the Flag* and wrote in 1896: "Defense of the flag has six figures with the central figure being the captain cheering his companions and holding high the union colors after a successful battle. The cruel ball wounds the lieutenant, who falls on the arm of his Captain. The drummer boy gently protects with one hand his wounded officer while the other has drawn his pistol ready to fire on the fleeing enemy. Back of the drummer Boy is an infantry-man ready to shoot while the trumpeter gives the signal to repose arms as the battle is won. The other figure is the wounded artilleryman."

On the southern side of *Defense of the Flag* stands a figure of a woman with her pen poised, writing "We write on page of granite what they wrought on field of battle." Named History but popularly known as Columbia, the figure was modeled on Triebel's wife, Santina. The title of the statue is *History Writing the Scroll of Fame*. A second casting of her can be found on the Mississippi State War Memorial Monument in Vicksburg.

The Soldier and Sailor's Monument was conceived by the Ladies Memorial Day Association of Peoria in 1892, because some people felt that interest in the sacrifices made during the Civil War was fading. One Peoria area unit, the 103rd Illinois Infantry Regiment, had 249 casualties, including nine officers and 240 enlisted. In 1893, Peoria native Fritz Triebel was contracted to do the sculpture. The monument is on the east side of the Peoria County Courthouse.

A large bundle of laurel wreaths, the symbol of victory, frames a banner with a dedicatory inscription: "Erected in memory of our heroes of 1861–1865 by the citizens of Peoria and Peoria County under the auspices of the Ladies Memorial Day Association." On either side of the base are bronze plaques naming the dead from the Peoria area. A bald eagle with an 11-foot wingspan is perched atop a globe at the top of the granite shaft. A tin box containing 1890s artifacts was placed inside the globe, and a copper box of similar items was buried in the granite base.

The Grand Army of the Republic Memorial Woods in River Forest was dedicated in 1930 after the Forest Preserve District extended Washington Boulevard through the Thatcher Woods Preserve and built the bridge crossing the Des Plaines River. It was dedicated by the Past President's Club of the Daughters of Union Veterans of the Civil War on October 27, 1930. The land was originally purchased for the Cook County Forest Preserve System in 1917.

The Grand Army of the Republic Memorial Woods features a memorial with an eagle on a stone clutching arrows at the end of a walkway with a flagpole. The plaque reads, "Grand Army of the Republic Memorial Woods, In honor of the men who wore the Blue and served in the Union Army of the Civil War USA 1861–1865. Greater love hath no man than this, that a man lay down his life for his friend."

The Rock Island Confederate Cemetery is the only surviving remnant of a massive prison camp that once held thousands of Confederate soldiers. Located on Arsenal Island in Rock Island, the cemetery is the final resting place for 1,950 prisoners of war who died in captivity from disease and poor living conditions at the camp. The burial plot is square and consists of 20 rows of graves running north-south. The spacing of each row is identical, but the beginning and end of the rows are irregular. In 1908, the Commission for Marking the Graves of Confederate Dead began to place distinctive pointed-top marble headstones inscribed with the name and regimental affiliation of each soldier on the graves. The graves were previously marked with wooden markers and private headstones. There is a paved walkway and a six-foot-tall obelisk the Daughters of the Confederacy dedicated in 2003 to the Confederate veterans who died at Rock Island. At the south end of the grounds is the cemetery's flagpole. Four Confederate cannons sit near the entrance, two each on either side of the monument. (Courtesy of the Department of Veterans Affairs, National Cemetery Administration.)

Three

The Spanish-American War

Here, the 1st Illinois Volunteer Infantry is departing Tampa, Florida, for Cuba. During its Spanish-American War tour of duty, the 1st Illinois Volunteer Infantry participated in the siege of Santiago. They were mustered into federal service on May 13, 1898. At that time, the regiment consisted of 50 officers and 979 enlisted. On June 5, the men arrived at Picnic Island in Tampa to wait for deployment to Cuba. The 1st Illinois arrived about two miles offshore from Siboney, Cuba, on July 8. On September 13, the regiment was given a 60-day furlough, and the men returned to Chicago. The members of the 1st Illinois were released from service on November 17, 1898. During its term of service, the regiment had 84 enlisted men die from disease, with nine more enlisted men being discharged on disability.

The McLean County Soldiers' and Sailors' Monument was dedicated May 30, 1913. The statue was designed to replace a Civil War monument erected in Franklin Park between 1868 and 1869, which was determined unsafe in 1914 due to the deterioration of its marble. The names from that earlier monument were incorporated into the plaques on this new memorial, which honors soldiers from the Civil, Black Hawk, Spanish-American, and Revolutionary Wars and the War of 1812. (Courtesy of Mark Werner.)

The monument consists of an ornamental arch with a shaft rising out of its roof. The arch has two doorways with a walk-through tunnel. Above each doorway is the figure of a soldier—one a Civil War soldier, pictured, and one a Spanish-American War soldier. The other two sides of the arch are each topped with an eagle. Another soldier stands atop the shaft. (Courtesy of Mark Werner.)

Over the years, the monument had items representing later wars added to it. On May 24, 1939, this World War I–era tank was placed at Bloomington's Miller Park to honor McLean County veterans who served in World War I. (Courtesy of Mark Werner.)

In 1949, the General Lawton Camp No. 7, United Spanish War Veterans, dedicated a Howitzer used during World War II to honor McLean County veterans who served in World War II. The inscription reads, "McLean County, in Loving and Grateful Remembrance of Valorous Deeds On Battlefield and Sea Dedicates This Monument as a Lasting Memorial to Her Sons and Citizens Who Freely Bared Their Breasts and Shed Their Life-Blood That Liberty and The Nation Might Endure That Oppression Should Fall and That Human Progress Might Advance." (Courtesy of Mark Werner.)

This naval cannon is a trophy of war captured by US forces from the Spanish cruiser *Vizcaya* at the famous Battle of Santiago Bay on July 3, 1898, a crucial engagement of the Spanish-American War. Less than one year later, at the request of local citizens and US congressman Robert Hitt, Galena received it by railcar. The cannon is nine feet long and weighs nearly five tons. The weapon was dedicated in Grant Park as part of the city's annual Grant Birthday Celebration on April 27, 1899, where it was to "be a display of public valor and virtue in all coming time." The cannon was rededicated in July 1899 through the efforts of the City of Galena, the Galena Foundation, and friends of Galena history.

Grand Army of the Republic Post No. 134 is pictured during the Lacon Memorial Day ceremony in 1920. The 7th Illinois Volunteer Infantry (1898–1898) was organized and mustered into service at Springfield on May 18, 1898, with 50 officers and 974 enlisted men. On June 3, the group was assigned to Second Brigade, Second Division, Second Army Corps at Camp Alger, Virginia, and remained there until being mustered out at Chicago on October 20, 1898, with 49 officers and 1,260 enlisted men. Two of the enlisted men died of disease and six deserted.

On September 3, 1928, the United Spanish War Veterans Camp 80 installed the Oak Park Spanish-American War Memorial. It was dedicated to honor those who served in the Spanish-American War, the Philippine Insurrection, and the Boxer Rebellion.

In November 1906, the proposal to build a Solders' and Sailors' Monument was on the ballot and was approved by the voters in Shelbyville during the general election. It was to be erected on the public square. In June 1908, the board appropriated $10,000 for the monument designed by Robert M. Root. The monument and four statuaries were to be the best medium Barre Vermont granite. The lower die and four corner columns were to be of the best dark Quincy granite. The monument consisted of a 35-foot-tall staff on top, an eight-foot bronze statue of a color bearer, and 24-foot-high flag staff, making a total height of 47 feet. Blake and Company of Chicago built the monument for $9,875. The dedication ceremonies were held on August 6, 1908.

On one side of the Solders' and Sailors' Monument in Shelbyville, between the six-foot-tall infantryman and the cavalryman, is inscribed, "Erected in 1907, in memory of the Soldiers and Sailors of Shelby County." A classic courthouse square monument, located in the square outside the Shelby County Courthouse, it was dedicated to the local soldiers and sailors of the Revolutionary War, War of 1812, Mexican War, Civil War, and Spanish-American War.

Opposite the inscription are six-foot-tall statues of a Navy sailor and an artilleryman. The dates of the beginning and end of the five wars (Revolutionary War, 1776–1781; War of 1812, 1812–1814; Mexican War, 1846–1848; Civil War, 1861–1865; and Spanish-American War, 1898–1899) are on another side. On each side of the shaft is a shield, which stands in bas-relief.

The 6th Illinois Volunteer Infantry saw service in Puerto Rico during the Spanish-American War. The National Guard regiment was mustered into federal service on May 11, 1898, in Springfield. Six days after being mustered, the regiment was sent to Camp Alger in Virginia. It was assigned to Second Army Corps. On July 8, the regiment was ordered to Cuba. While en route, the Spanish troops around Santiago surrendered, so on July 21, the regiment was redirected to Puerto Rico. On September 7, 1898, the regiment left Puerto Rico and on November 25 was mustered out.

Four

World War I

This large piece of German artillery, nicknamed "Big Bertha," was captured by the 33rd Infantry Division in Somme, France, during World War I. (Courtesy of the National Archives.)

The 1st Infantry Regiment of the Illinois National Guard is pictured leaving its home armory in Chicago in 1917. The unit was mustered into service on April 4, 1917, and drafted into service on August 5, 1917. On October 12, 1917, it was redesignated the 131st Infantry Regiment and assigned to the 33rd Division. On May 30, 1918, Colonel Sanborn arrived in France with the 131st Infantry Regiment. The regiment participated in the Somme and Meuse-Argonne offensives between August 8 and November 11, 1918. On June 6, 1919, they were demobilized at Camp Grant in Illinois. (Courtesy of the International Film Service, Chicago.)

On August 4, 1918, the 131st Infantry Regiment was entrenched outside the town of Albert, France, and needed intelligence on the enemy's strength. On his own accord, Sgt. James B. Powers of Company L went forward alone to accomplish this task. Though harassed by enemy snipers the whole way, he successfully made it through the town and to Allied forces dug in on the other side. His reconnaissance provided valuable information that benefited the commanders. American and British forces prepared for an assault on Albert. The mission entailed securing the major roads that intersected inside the town. Control of these roads allowed the Allies to move supplies into the Somme offensive combat zone. The coming battle would be the third the citizens of Albert had endured in two years, having been taken and retaken by both sides repeatedly. The Third Battle of Albert began on August 21, 1918; within a day of hard fighting, the Allies had achieved victory. For his extraordinary heroism under fire in accomplishing his mission, Powers received the Distinguished Service Cross.

The Belleau Wood Second Division Memorial was erected by the Second Division Association on June 5, 1926. Col. Hanford MacNider, assistant secretary of war, delivered the dedicatory address at the unveiling of the monument in Des Plaines to commemorate the Second Division's service in the world war. The memorial marks the renaming of the preserve to Belleau Wood, after the famed battle in France in June 1918. The memorial is a long, narrow, elliptically shaped slab featuring the painted insignia of the Second Division. The battle lasted most of the month of June 1918 and cost US forces more than 9,000 killed and wounded. Several small metal plaques were added across the top of the memorial marking its rededication in 1977 to honor locals from the Second Division who served in World War II and the Korean War.

On May 12, 2009, the Northwest Suburban Detachment, Marine Corps League, dedicated a separate memorial boulder with a plaque to honor the particular role of the US Marine Corps in the Battle of Belleau Wood. The first monument, erected in the years following the end of World War I, honors the US Army 2nd Division, which the 4th Marine Brigade was part of; however, nothing on the monument reflects that. The plaque reads, "Belleau Wood—June 1918. The Marines Didn't Win The War Here. But They Saved The Allies From Defeat. (Lt. Gen. R.L. Bullard, US Army) / Dedicated to the Marines and Corpsmen of the 4th Brigade, 2nd Division, AEF. (A little raft of sea soldiers in an ocean of the Army.)" This battle is generally credited with saving Paris from the advancement of the German army.

The Forest Park Soldiers, Sailors, and Marines World War I Memorial was dedicated in 1924 by members of the Kiwanis Club of Forest Park in front of the original Village Hall. In the 1960s, it was moved to the library grounds and later to its current location by the Forest Park American Legion Post 105 and the Village of Forest Park.

The memorial features a large granite boulder with an attached copper relief depicting a soldier being comforted. A second plaque has the following inscription: "In memory of those who have sacrificed all in the World War—presented by the Kiwanis Club of Forest Park, IL." Rising high over the monument is the US flag.

This vintage postcard, postmarked 1928, depicts the Soldiers, Sailors, and Marines Memorial in its original location. Both plaques are visible, although the details are difficult to see. There was no flagpole on the original memorial.

The Village of Forest Park Police Department Color Guard participates in the Veteran's Day ceremony and wreath laying, hosted by members of the American Legion and village officials at Popelka Park on November 11, 2017. Popelka Park is the current location of the memorial.

The Herrin Doughboy was originally erected in September 6, 1927, at the intersection of Park Avenue and Monroe Street. It was moved to a temporary location near the Herrin American Legion in 1956 and found a permanent home in Herrin City Park in 1964. In 2002, the doughboy made his way back to the downtown plaza area across from city hall. A major portion of the move was handled by the National Guard. The plaques honoring veterans were also moved and placed on the wall behind the doughboy. The memorial includes a granite base, bronze plaques, and a bronze statue of a doughboy. The inscription on the front plaque reads, "In Memory of our Heroic Dead Veterans of the World War 1917–1918." It is followed by 55 names in two columns, with stars designating the 21 who were killed or died in service. Under the plaque are emblems of the Army, Navy, Marine, and nurse corps. The inscription on a rear plaque reads, "In Memory of our Heroic Veterans of World War II 1945," followed by 45 names in two columns. It then reads, "These Men Were Killed in Action or Died in Service."

NATIONAL JEWISH WAR MEMORIAL — OAKRIDGE JEWISH CEMETERY — HILLSIDE, ILL.

The National Jewish War Memorial and Military Burial Plot in Oakridge Jewish Cemetery is located in Hillside. The memorial and plot commemorate the services rendered to the United States by its Jewish citizens in periods of national emergency. The memorial was dedicated on September 8, 1940, by the American Legion Yarmo-DeVere Post 469, American Legion Auxiliary and Yarmo-DeVere Squadron, Sons of American Legion. The original ceremony and appropriate commemorative program was held to mark the first time that national recognition was given publicly to Americans of Jewish faith who served the United States in periods of national emergency and war.

The Hines Dilboy statue depicts a soldier of Hellenic American ancestry. George Dilboy was the first Greek to die in World War I, in a battle near Belleau, France. Dilboy, who was born in Lachata, Asia Minor, in 1896, came with his family to America in 1916. Shortly after joining the New Hampshire National Guard, war broke out, and he was assigned to Company H, 103rd Infantry, 26th Division. He was sent to France. In a battlefield near Belleau, Dilboy accompanied his platoon leader to reconnoiter the grounds. As he advanced, Dilboy was fired upon by an enemy machine-gun nest. He stood on nearby railroad tracks and opened fire but failed to silence the gun. Dilboy rushed with his bayonet fixed and fell within 25 yards of the gun. Though his body was bullet ridden, he managed to shoot and kill two of the enemy and disperse the rest before he died. He was awarded the Congressional Medal of Honor posthumously. (Courtesy of Daniel DuVerney, Hines Media Service.)

The George Dilboy statue was dedicated on May 24, 1942. It depicts Pfc. George Dilboy standing in a World War I Army uniform, deep-set eyes looking outward, watching, a rifle held in his hands. Since 1942, this soldier has never left his post and remains at the entrance of the Hines Veterans Administration Hospital. George Dilboy volunteered to fight in the US Army in the Mexican Border War during 1916 and 1917. He was honorably discharged but later rejoined the US Army and served in the 26th Division in France during World War I. Dilboy became the first Greek American to be awarded the Medal of Honor. He was 22 years old. The young hero was buried in Lachata, but during the Greek-Turkish War, the United States requested that his ashes be sent to Arlington National Cemetery. Hines was chosen as the site of the statue and center for a George Dilboy foundation, since it is situated within a government reservation where perpetual care could be given. The foundation was established in 1934 by Chicago's Hellenic Post 343. The program was developed by Costos P. Mellas, 87, a former Maywood resident. (Courtesy of Daniel DuVerney, Hines Media Service.)

This statue of a World War I doughboy stands on the grounds at Hines Veterans Administration Hospital, near Maywood, in honor of Pfc. George Dilboy. The inscription reads, "George Dilboy, Born Feb. 5, 1896, Alachata, Asia Minor. Killed in action near Belleau Woods, France, July 18 1918. Pvt. 1st Cl. Co. H 103rd Inf. 26th Div. U. S. Army A. E. F. Posthumously awarded the Congressional Medal of Honor 'For Gallantry and Intrepidity in Action and Beyond the Call of Duty.' " The inscription continues, "From far Ionia he came a new American true to his Hellenic ancestry to fight and die for country and liberty under the Stars and Stripes. George Dilboy Chapter No. 13 DAV of WW under the Auspices of the George Dilboy Memorial Foundation, Costas P. Mellas, President."

The Carroll County Circle of Lanark World War I Honor Roll is located in the Lanark City Cemetery and list the names of local heroes who served during World War I. The star indicates those killed in action. It was dedicated and installed by the City of Lanark and the American Legion Post 357.

The Lanark World War I Veterans Memorial is dedicated to Lanark's honored servicemen who served from 1917 to 1919. This monument was donated by Col. H.H. Wilson, who served in the US Air Force. It is located in the Lanark City Cemetery.

Morton Grove's doughboy statue was dedicated on July 31, 1921, by the Women's War Working Circle as a tribute to those from Morton Grove who fought in World War I, from the United States' entry in 1917 through the end of the war in 1918. The Women's War Working Circle was a group of volunteers who worked with the Red Cross to support soldiers during World War I. They raised funds to commission the statue and purchase the land that the doughboy sits upon today by organizing a festival and carnival.

As the decades passed, the statue began to show its age, and the concrete base was also in need of restoration. A restoration company was hired to restore the statue and the base. On September 24, 2017, outside the Morton Grove Public Library, the village unveiled the refurbished World War I doughboy statue. The memorial honors veterans who served in "The War to End All Wars." The festival, originally organized to raise money to fund the memorial, became the first of what is known today as Morton Grove Days.

The St. Adalbert World War I Monument is dedicated to the Polish American veterans who fought in World War I. The memorial, located in St. Adalbert Cemetery in Niles, was designed by an unidentified sculptor and was dedicated in 1928. It is a war monument honoring Marines, Army, Navy, and Haller's Army of 20,000 Polish Americans. Many of the soldiers listed on the monument were members of the Illinois National Guard's 33rd Infantry Division or units subordinate to it.

There is, and historically has been, a large Polish population in the city of Chicago and its surrounding suburbs. Niles is just north of Chicago, and St. Adalbert Cemetery is located there. The Archdiocese of Chicago consecrated it in 1872 to serve the city's Poles; in terms of burials, it is the largest within the archdiocese.

Poles supported the Allies during World War I because they lost their nation in the late 18th century, having been absorbed by the Ukraine, Germany, and Russia. They won back their independence in 1918, only to suffer terribly at the hands of the Nazis 21 years later. During the Cold War, Poland was a client state under the control of the Soviet Union. Poland is now a close ally of America and, coincidently, is the Illinois National Guard's partner in the Partnership for Peace program. The Illinois National Guard and the Polish army have conducted ongoing joint missions in both Afghanistan and Iraq.

After World War I, the Polish American volunteers who served within Haller's Army were not recognized as veterans by either the American or Polish governments. This led to friction between the Polish community in the United States and the Polish government and resulted in the subsequent refusal by Polish Americans to again help the Polish cause militarily. An estimated 20,000 Polish persons answered the call to fight for freedom and the opportunity to regain Poland's independence during World War I in the Polish army in France (Armia Polska we Francyi). They were recruited from among the Polish immigrants in America to fight with France. The Polish Army in France was also called Haller's Army, after the general who commanded it, or the Blue Army, for the blue uniforms the soldiers wore.

The Oak Park–River Forest World War I Memorial, *Peace Triumphant*, commemorates those from Oak Park and River Forest who served during the First World War. The dedication ceremony was held on Armistice Day, November 11, 1925. United States vice president Charles Gates Dawes and Gen. John J. Pershing were present for its dedication. It is estimated that around 12,000 people attended the dedication ceremonies. Residents raised almost $60,000 to pay for the monument's construction and upkeep. This bronze and granite memorial was designed by Gilbert P. Riswold. The figure of Columbia sheathing her sword represents the war's end.

The base of the monument states: "Erected by the citizens of Oak Park and River Forest, Illinois, in honor of the men of this community who took part in the World War 1914–1918." The total height of the monument is 21 feet, 3 inches. Columbia, armed but representing peace by sheathing her sword, is the dominant feature. Bronze life-sized statues of a soldier, sailor, and airman are in the front. A tablet, 5 feet wide and 15 feet high, lists the names of the 56 local men who fell in battle in World War I plus the 2,446 others who served. Among them is the name "Hemingway, E.M." Oak Park–born Ernest Hemingway served as an ambulance driver and later immortalized his experiences in *A Farewell to Arms*. The bronze work was done by Jules Berchem & Son.

The Peoria County World War I and World War II Memorial in Peoria was dedicated on May 26, 2007. The memorial was dedicated by the county board and a memorial committee and funded by private citizens and companies. It honors those from the area who served in World Wars I and II. The memorial is made of a gray granite column sculpted to look like a Roman numeral "I." A black granite plaque is engraved: "Peoria County Veterans who lost their lives in the line of duty during World War One." It then lists the following information: "World War One, United States Involvement, 1917–1918; Peoria County, total service members, 5,500, lost lives, 211; United States, total service members, 4,734,991; Battle deaths, 53,402; other service deaths (non theater), 63,114; non mortal wounded, 204,002." Also listed are the names of all of the service members killed in action.

The River Grove World War I Memorial was dedicated in 1920 by the River Grove American Legion Post 335 and the Village of River Grove. Originally placed in front of the American Legion Post 335 building on Grand Avenue, it was moved to its current location at St. Joseph Catholic Cemetery and rededicated. Originally, the monument paid homage to the 25 residents from the Leyden area who made the ultimate sacrifice during the First World War. But now, the double eagle, white marble monument stands watch over veterans from several wars.

The Wauconda Township World War I Memorial was dedicated by the Wauconda American Legion Post, the Wauconda Park District, and the Village of Wauconda in 1926. It is located in Memorial Park. The memorial, a brass plaque on a gray granite slab, features three flags and several benches.

Five

World War II

On March 5, 1941, the 33rd Infantry Division, from the Illinois National Guard, was inducted into federal service for a year's training at Camp Forrest, Tennessee. This photograph shows the 108th Quartermaster Regiment during induction ceremonies at the Northwest Armory in Chicago. The 33rd Infantry Division and all its subordinate units ended up serving in the United States, Africa, Europe, and the Pacific for the rest of World War II. (Photograph by ACME Newspictures Inc.)

This is a life-sized memorial to S.Sgt. Donald E. Hurst, who served during World War II, the Cold War, and the Korean Conflict. From 1944 to 1946, he served as a B-17 waist gunner in the US Army Air Corps, 8th Air Force, the 303rd and 305th Bomber Group stationed in England. From 1947 to 1957, he served onboard B-29 bombers as a member of the 15th Air Force assigned to the Strategic Air Command. The sculpture was cast at Wagner Foundry in Chicago and dedicated on May 18, 2018. In 1944, fifteen-year-old Don Hurst enlisted in the US Army Air Corps. After completing his training as an aerial gunner, Hurst was sent overseas to the European theater. On February 9, 1945, while flying his 12th mission in a B-17G Flying Fortress, his plane was shot down. He helped eight of the severely injured crewmen to safety and used his .50-caliber machine gun to fight off the Germans.

Since 1942, this small western suburb of Chicago has marked the second Sunday in September as Maywood Bataan Day. The residents were then calling attention to the over 100 Maywood National Guard troops who were taken prisoner when American forces surrendered at Bataan on April 9, 1942. These men endured the death march, prison camps, "Hell ships," and eventual slave labor in Japan. The men were part of Company B, 192nd Tank Battalion. The original Maywood Bataan Day drew more than 100,000 spectators, dozens of marching bands, and celebrities, including Chicago mayor Ed Kelley and movie and radio stars. Today's celebration is much smaller but still draws several hundred people. The memorial is supported by the Village of Maywood and a nonprofit group, the Maywood Bataan Day Organization, which in 1999 had the local park dedicated as Veterans Memorial Park. Ironically, the memorial park in Maywood is bordered by a commuter rail track that now runs trains by Nippon Sharyo, a Japanese railcar manufacturer that used Maywood POWs as wartime slave labor.

Maywood's annual Bataan Day Service is the longest and largest continual World War II memorial event in the Chicago area. The service has included a concert of musical pieces and color guard presentations. Pictured are the armaments that commemorate the 192nd Tank Battalion.

This tank was dedicated in 1946 and was located at the Maywood American Legion Post until Veterans Memorial Park was created in 1999. The plaque reads, "In memory of our Illinois comrades of the 192nd Tank Battalion who gave their lives in the service of their country on Bataan, and in Japanese Prisoner of War camps" and lists the names of the 56 heroes who were killed in action.

Maywood was the home of the Illinois National Guard 33rd Tank Company (Company B). It was organized on May 3, 1929. On November 25, 1940, Company B's 122 men were inducted into active service and became part of the 192nd Tank Battalion, which fought on the Philippine Islands. The unit became part of the notorious Bataan Death March in April 1942. Only 41 men returned to Maywood alive.

In recognition of the enormous sacrifice endured by members of the 192nd Tank Battalion and to honor the soldiers from Maywood who died on the Bataan Death March, Congress designated Maywood the "Village of Eternal Light." The tank and cannon are part of Veterans Memorial Park. The cannon is a British BL 60-pounder Mk I, mounted on a Mk II carriage with tractor wheels.

The Mokena M-5 Anti-Tank Gun Memorial is a restored M-5 anti-tank gun used during the Second World War. It is located in the Pioneer Memorial Cemetery in Mokena and dedicated to the men and women of the armed services of the United States. The gun was requested by the Mokena AmVets. It arrived in 1948, and its transportation was funded by the Mokena Civic Association. In 2017, the M-5 Anti-Tank Gun Memorial was refurbished by veteran and patriot volunteers from the Veterans Garage on behalf of William F. Martin VFW Post 275. A rededication ceremony was held on Veterans Day, November 11, 2017. (Courtesy of Ramona Machay.)

This photograph shows service members' tombstones in Pioneer Memorial Cemetery and part of the Mokena M-5 Anti-Tank Gun Memorial. (Courtesy of Ramona Machay.)

The Mokena Veterans Memorial is located in St. Joseph Cemetery in Mokena. It was installed on May 30, 1946, by the William F. Martin VFW Post 275 and is dedicated to those who served in the armed forces. (Courtesy of Ramona Machay.)

The World War II Polish American Katyn Monument, near the entrance of St. Adalbert's Cemetery in Niles, is one of the best-known memorials. Historically, there has been a large Polish population in the city of Chicago and its surrounding suburbs. In 1940, over 20,000 Poles, many of them military officers and policemen who had supported and fought for the Allies during World War I, were massacred by Stalin's secret police in the Katyn Forest in western Russia.

This sculpture depicts Mary holding a bound Polish army officer killed during the massacre. On April 10, 2010, the wounds of the atrocity were reopened when Polish president Lech Kaczyski, along with many of Poland's highest military and civilian leaders, were killed in a plane crash while approaching Smolensk Air Base in Russia. They were on their way to attend a ceremony marking the 70th anniversary of the massacre.

This brass relief depicts the atrocities that were committed during World War II in the Katyn Forest in western Russia. It reads, "Dedicated to the martyrdom of Poles who gave their lives for the Fatherland—Hostages of the war slain in 1940 by the Soviet NKVD. Officers of the Polish army, spiritual leaders, intelligentsia, police officers, soldiers and border patrol shot in Katyn and other areas of the inhumane Soviet territory."

The Peoria County World War II Memorial was dedicated in Peoria on May 26, 2007, by the county board and a memorial committee and was funded by private citizens and companies. It honors those from the area who served in World War II. The memorial is made of two gray granite columns sculpted to look like the Roman numeral II. A black granite plaque is engraved: "Peoria County Veterans who lost their lives in the line of duty during World War Two." Also listed are the names of all of the service members killed in action.

The Village of River Grove World War II Veterans Memorial was erected by the American Legion Post and Village of River Grove in 1945. The monument is made of polished gray granite with an ornate brass plaque. The memorial and the 75-mm Pack Howitzer used in World War II were rededicated by the Central Leyden VFW Post 5979 and the American Legion Post 335 on May 30, 1978.

The River Forest World Wars Memorial was dedicated by the River Forest Service Club and the Village of River Forest on Memorial Day 1948 in honor of the men and women of River Forest who served in the world wars. In October 2009, a Boy Scout from Troop 66 had a walkway made of memorial bricks dedicated to World War I and World War II veterans installed as his Eagle Scout project. The memorial features a granite monument with an eagle engraved into it, benches, and the US flag. Annually, the River Forest Service Club and the Village of River Forest have conducted a Memorial Day parade. This parade recognizes and honors the men and women who are serving or who have served in the armed forces of the United States and especially those who gave their lives in serving. Grand marshals have included officers from Great Lakes, including admirals, a World War II ace fighter pilot, and other dignitaries.

The Hero Street USA Monument in Silvis features a 17.5-foot-tall, 35-ton sculpture of a bronze eagle clutching a flag and a rifle atop a memorial honoring the 100 people from this one block-long street who have volunteered to serve in the US military since World War II. In particular, the eight men from this historically Mexican community who made the ultimate sacrifice during World War II are honored. Second Street was renamed Hero Street USA. The Illinois State Historical Society marker reads, "Hero Street, USA. received its name in 1968 to honor the fifty-seven servicemen from thirty-three families on this block-and-a-half who served in defense of America between 1941 and 1968. Six men died in World War II and two in the Korean Conflict. Some families sent as many as six or seven sons; some men served in both wars. At the date of the erection of this marker, over 110 men and women from this small area had served in the United States Armed Services." It was erected in 1989 by the City of Silvis and the Illinois State Historical Society.

The Wauconda World War II Memorial was dedicated on October 14, 1948, by the Wauconda American Legion Post, the Wauconda Park District, and the Village of Wauconda to those who served during the Second World War. It is located in Memorial Park. The memorial is a brass plaque on a gray granite slab.

Six

The Korean War and the Vietnam War

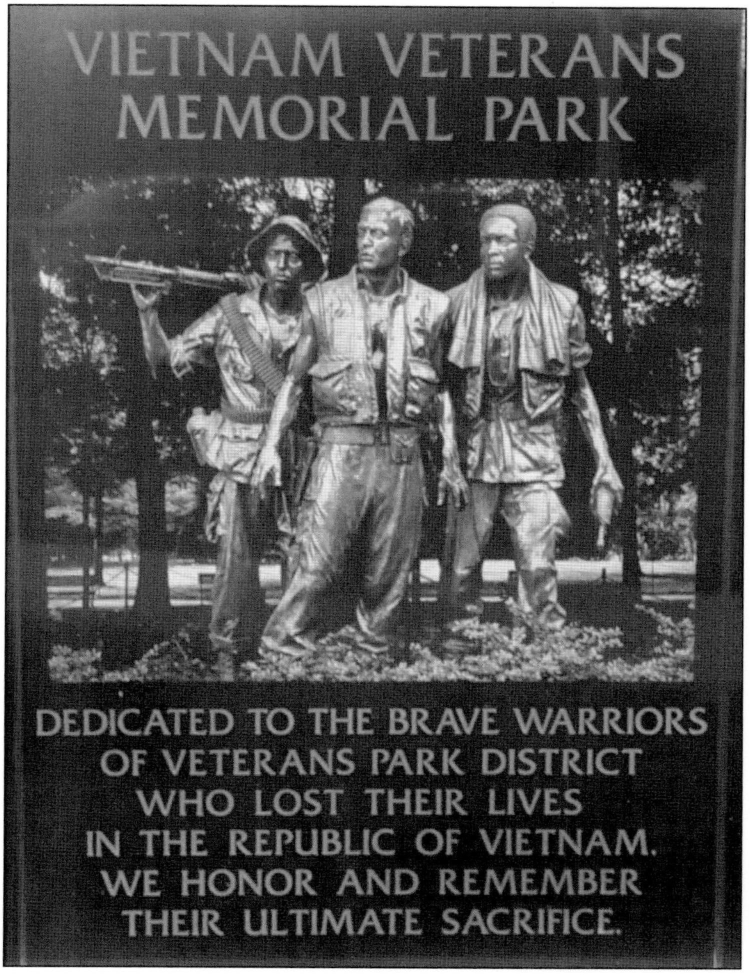

The Korean and Vietnam Wars were the two most unpopular wars in US history. Unfortunately, those who bore the worst of the wars, the service members, were abandoned by their government and the population when they returned to a nation in turmoil. Since the 1990s, much has been done to right this wrong, but much is left to be done. Many of these veterans were cheated out of a hero's welcome home.

The Robert E. Wurtsbaugh Memorial Bridge is located in Ellsworth Park in Danville. It is dedicated to the first casualty of the Korean War from Vermilion County. He was a private first class assigned to the 5th Marine Regiment, 1st Marine Division. The memorial was erected and dedicated on May 30, 1989. The Robert E. Wurtsbaugh marker is on the left by the footbridge. During the Korean War, 23 service people from Vermilion County were killed.

The Monument to Peace was donated to the Village of Elmwood Park by the Elmwood Park Fourth of July Committee on July 4, 1980. With the Vietnam War having ended five years earlier, peace was welcomed. The 36-foot-high, 2.5-ton stainless steel sculpture was designed and constructed by Jack F. Gron. The sword and the shield are symbols of man's earliest conflicts. The slashes represent the ravages of battle, suggesting that they are damaged and cannot be used again.

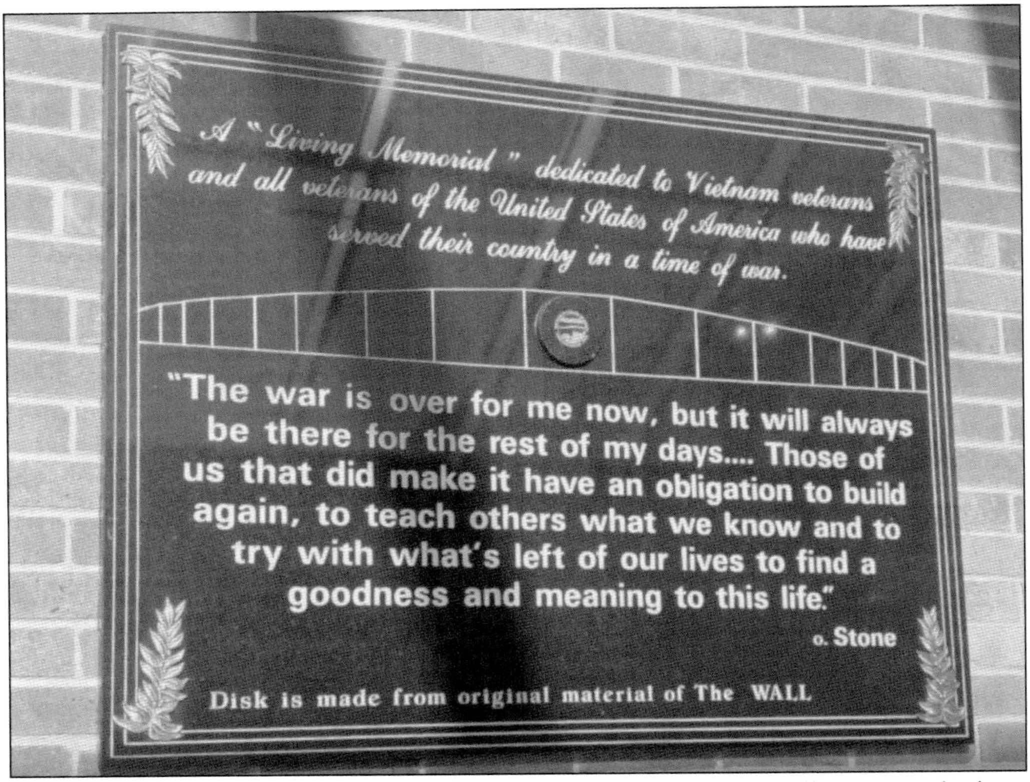

The Vietnam Veterans Memorial was dedicated on August 22, 1995, to all veterans who have served their country in a time of war. (Courtesy of Daniel DuVerney, Hines Media Service.)

The following organizations contributed to the memorial: Hines Hospital Social Work Service; 4th BN, 12th Marines, 3rd Marine Division; Elite Forces Chapter of 173rd Airborne; Chapter 6 Polish Legion of American Veterans; Kosciuszko Post No. 30 Polish Legion of American Veterans; USA Vietnam Veterans of America Chicago, Northwest Chapter 209. (Courtesy of Daniel DuVerney, Hines Media Service.)

The Vietnam Veterans Memorial Park is located in Melrose Park on the Victory Centre of River Woods assisted living campus. It was dedicated on July 27, 2016, to the 16 veterans from the area who died in Vietnam. The Village of Melrose Park donated the land and installed most of the infrastructure, such as the pavement and the retaining wall, and the Veterans Park District agreed to do all the landscaping and maintenance for the property. The dedication ceremony included a presentation of the colors and a rifle salute by American Legion Franklin Park Post 974 and American Legion Post 888 from Northlake, a benediction by Deacon Ray Behrendt from Sacred Heart Parish in Melrose Park, and renditions of the national anthem and "God Bless America" by Gianna Capra Uroni.

The Morton Grove American Legion Memorial Civic Center consists of the building, flags, cannon, plaques dedicated to the services, and a plaque on a granite rock. The plaque states, "The American Legion Memorial, Built in 1949 by Morton Grove Post 134 of the American Legion Dept. of Illinois. This has been the post's home and base for veterans of military service of all eras to work together and provide help to their comrades and others with needs. The memorial is dedicated to Morton Grove heroes who made the Supreme Sacrifice serving our Nation's military." The memorial was rededicated in 1982 to include casualties of Vietnam.

The Morton Grove Veterans' Living Memorial contains 20 trees that surround a brick wall. There are several plaques; one is mounted on the wall, another on a granite boulder in the grove. It was dedicated and installed by the Village of Morton Grove and its park district. The plaque on the boulder reads, "This grove dedicated in 1976 . . . to honor all who served Jan 1, 1961–Sept 30, 1975."

The Morton Grove Veterans' Living Memorial was rededicated, and a plaque was placed on the wall. This plaque reads, "This living memorial grove of trees stands in honor of those from Morton Grove who gave their lives serving their Country." It then lists the veterans killed in every conflict since the Civil War. It further states, "Dedicated November 11, 1995. The memorial commemorates the service of all Veterans and recognizes their unity in the sacrifices they made for our Country."

The 126th Supply and Service Company of Quincy was the only National Guard unit in the state of Illinois called upon to fight in Vietnam. The unit was alerted on May 13, 1968, that it would be going to Vietnam. The men were first sent to Fort Carson, Colorado, by train and bus. In September 1968, a total of 129 guardsmen of the Illinois National Guard arrived in Chu Lai, South Vietnam, where they were assigned to the 23rd Supply and Transportation Battalion, Americal Division. The 126th included nine sets of brothers, including Joe and Dick Koetters, both lifelong residents of Quincy. The 126th's primary job was delivering jet fuel to landing zones; however, it was also responsible for overseeing the transportation and issuance of the battalion's food, clothing, fuel, equipment, and vehicles. The unit picked up the nickname "Hallmark" because the United States "cared enough to send the very best" (the 126th). The 126th returned from Vietnam and was released from active federal service on August 19, 1969, with every man it left with alive and well.

The Village of River Grove Korean Veterans Memorial is a black granite memorial that has both North and South Korea engraved on it. It reads, "America's Forgotten War Korea 1950–1953" and lists all of the units that served there. The dedication states, "In grateful appreciation to those who gave from their hearts to make this memorial, Chairman Louis De Angelis, Co-Chairman John Drent. Dedicated this 19th day of June 1993."

The Village of River Grove Vietnam Veterans Memorial was dedicated on Memorial Day, May 30, 1988. The polished black granite memorial has the dates 1959 and 1975 on either side of five stars, representing the five branches of the US military.

The Women Veterans Memorial, dedicated on August 18, 2001, is located in the Rock Island National Cemetery. Phyllis Dolin, a retired Air Force colonel, personally paid for the memorial to honor the over 1.8 million women who have served in America's armed forces. Dolin retired from the Air Force in 1985 after 26 years of service. The memorial is an obelisk of gray granite, four feet tall and three feet wide at its base. Inscriptions recognize women who have served all of the uniformed branches. Flagpoles stand at each point of the floral star. Each side of the stone obelisk is dedicated to various branches of the military.

The Stephenson County Vietnam War Memorial was dedicated on May 25, 1987, by the VietNow Freeport Chapter and Stephenson County. The memorial is "dedicated to those lost during the Vietnam Era" and includes the names of soldiers who died and one who is missing. It consists of a black granite stone topped with the battlefield cross of a helmet, rifle, and combat boots. The back of the memorial reads: "Remembered are the more than 58,000 killed the 303,704 wounded, the 2456 still missing . . . 102 from Illinois. The over 60,000 to date, who could no longer live with the memory of the war and ended their own lives. And the men and women of Stephenson Co. who served proudly during the Vietnam era." (Both, courtesy of Sgt. David Davies.)

The Washington Veteran's Memorial was initiated by a Boy Scout working on his Eagle Scout project in 2004. A plaque reads, "In Honor and Memory of US Veterans." This memorial is for all US veterans and features the US flag, flags of all the services, memorial bricks, inspirational veteran quotes, and, as the centerpiece, a Huey Cobra helicopter with a placard describing the purpose of the helicopter and specific information about the service of the Cobra in the memorial. The AH-1 Cobras were developed for use by the Army during the Vietnam War. They were used in every major engagement from the Tet offensive in 1968 to the end of the war. Cobras provided fire support for ground forces, escorted transport helicopters, served as aerial rocket artillery battalions in the two Airmobile divisions, and other roles.

Seven

Combined Memorials

This sign in Park Ridge serves to remind people that freedom and the American way of life has a sobering price. The lives given in pursuit of and belief of American freedoms have included: French and Indian War, 2,200; Revolutionary War, 29,435; War of 1812, 20,000; Mexican-American War, 13,283; Civil War, 623,026; Spanish-American War, 2,446; World War I, 116,708; World War II, 407,316; Korean War, 36,914; Vietnam War, 58,151; Desert Storm, 269; and the Global War on Terrorism, over 6,000.

Pictured above is Mary Ludwig Hays, also known as Molly Pitcher. As was customary at the time, she accompanied her husband, William Hays, when he enlisted as a gunner in the Continental Army. On June 28, 1778, they found themselves in the Battle of Monmouth. Under the ongoing barrage of British fire, Mary is said to have carried spring water to the men on the artillery line to quench their thirst and cool their overheated cannons. When her husband collapsed in the 100-degree heat, she took over for him, competently firing in his place. Because of her honorable actions in battle, years later the Honorable Order of Molly Pitcher was established and is bestowed by the Field Artillery and Air Defense Artillery Associations to recognize women who have voluntarily contributed in a significant way to the artillery communities. Pictured below is Lauren Fiorentino, a recipient of the Honorable Order of Molly Pitcher, for her tireless efforts with the Family Readiness Group.

The Assyrian American War Memorial features one central panel with an inscription and dedication names and two longer side panels with additional dedication names. There are three flagpoles behind each side panel, which are used to fly the flags of each branch of service, and one central flagpole with American and POW/MIA flags. Additionally, there are brick tiles in front of the monument with dedication names.

The Assyrian American War Memorial, dedicated on May 16, 1998, by the Assyrian American AmVets Post 5, is located in Elmwood Cemetery in River Grove. It was dedicated to honor members of the Assyrian community who gave their lives serving the United States. The panels are made of smooth gray granite, weigh about 16,000 pounds, and bear the names of 500 Assyrian Americans from the Chicago region who as young men were sent to serve their country. This memorial marker, written in Assyrian, commemorates an Assyrian American who died for the United States during the "War of 1914–1918."

The Bartlett Veterans Memorial features a statue of a soldier mourning a fallen comrade as the focal point and includes four memorial benches, an American flag, a flag for each branch of the military, and a walkway with bricks engraved with the names of donors. The Veterans of Foreign Wars, American Legion, and Village of Bartlett supported the veterans memorial to honor members of the armed forces. Phase one began in 2007, and a dedication ceremony was held on May 26, 2010. The sculpture was designed by Greg Martin, a member of the American Legion Post 1212. The Bartlett Veterans Memorial, dedicated on May 26, 2012, aims to make visitors acutely aware of two ideas: "Freedom isn't free" and "All gave some; some gave all."

The Chatham Veterans Memorial on the Square was dedicated in 1862. It features a cannon that was cast in 1862 and was a gift of Ben F. Caldwell, former congressman and resident of Chatham. Over time, the cannon and carriage deteriorated. The American Legion, with the support of members of the community, built a new memorial incorporating the cannon. Renovations were funded by community and private donations, and the memorial was rededicated in June 1942. In 1990, the village put a flower garden around the memorial, and in the fall, yellow ribbons were placed in the evergreen trees to show support for the troops during Operation Desert Storm. In November 1999, memorial bricks were added. It was rededicated on November 11, 2000, by the Village of Chatham, American Legion Post 759, and VFW Post 4763. The plaque reads, "To honor all US service men and women who served in war and peace in defense of our freedom."

The Italian American War Memorial was dedicated by the Old Neighborhood Italian American Club in 2008. The memorial is dedicated to those Italian American veterans who made the ultimate sacrifice: "Gold Star family members always remembered." The Peter Troost Monument Company designed and erected this beautiful memorial, located in front of the Italian American Club in Chicago. It is made of polished black and gray granite and features a granite eagle perched atop the center pedestal. The gray panels have the emblem of each branch of military service engraved on them. On the polished black granite pedestal is engraved the US Flag, the POW/MIA emblem, and the quote, "Dedicated to the men and women of the Armed Forces, past, present and future." Above the memorial flies the US, Italian, POW/MIA, and several organizational flags.

In November 2013, a second part was added to the Italian American War Memorial and it was once again dedicated by the Old Neighborhood Italian American Club. The addition to the memorial honors all veterans. The polished black granite slab is engraved with the US flag and the emblems of the military branches and POW/MIA. In front of the memorial are engraved bricks dedicated to the memory of Italian Americans who served.

The Lake Park Memorial Pavilion was dedicated in June 1975. It was expanded and rededicated on July 18, 2004, by the VFW Post 2992, the American Legion Post 36, and the City of Des Plaines. The memorial honors the men and women of Des Plaines who have served in the armed forces, from the Civil War to the present day. It features an engraved memorial brick walkway that leads to the pavilion, a wall displaying emblems representing five military branches, panels honoring service members and the conflicts that they served in, including monuments dedicated after the Civil War, the Spanish-American War, and World War I. Another monument commemorates the hosting of the Vietnam Veterans' Moving Memorial Wall, July 2–7, 1988.

On November 11, 2015, Chillicothe veterans broke ground on a new memorial for American service members. Chillicothe Veterans Memorial honors all veterans, living and deceased, from the Revolutionary War to the War on Terror. It is meant to serve as a reminder of the contributions that service members have made throughout America's history. The Chillicothe Veterans Memorial was dedicated on July 4, 2016, on the 240th anniversary of our nation's birth. The memorial features a long wall that reads, "Freedom Is Not Free;" red bricks in the shape of a star and engraved with names and memories of veterans past and present; flagpoles; benches; a battlefield cross; and statues. The battlefield cross is symbolic of fallen service members. (Courtesy of Michael A. Holub.)

This statue represents a Revolutionary War–era soldier, who epitomizes the notion of the citizen soldier. (Courtesy of Michael A. Holub.)

This statue represents a modern-day combat soldier, giving homage to the citizen soldier and the professional soldier. This statue faces the Revolutionary War–era one. (Courtesy of Michael A. Holub.)

The Elmhurst Veterans Memorial, originally dedicated on May 30, 1977, has a brass plaque that reads, "For God, and country and the memory of those who gave their lives in freedom's name, T.H.B. Post 187 American Legion rededicates its efforts." It was rededicated on Memorial Day 1993. The veterans memorial is dedicated to all US veterans who have honorably served this country. It features memorial markers for World War II, Vietnam, Cold War, and Gulf War veterans. Additionally, flags from each branch of service fly in front of gray granite structures engraved with the corresponding service crest. A brass plaque on a granite slab reads, "In perpetual memory of our comrades who served the United States of America in its wars by members of the Veterans of Foreign Wars." Also inscribed on each granite structure are the name of the war and the number of service members who died in each war. At the base of each granite structure is a quote from past leaders.

The Franklin Park Veteran's Memorial was dedicated on November 11, 2000, by the Village of Franklin Park and the Franklin Park American Legion Post 974. Any individual who has resided in Franklin Park and served in any branch of the military is eligible to have his or her name listed on the memorial. There are pillars for each branch of service with corresponding flags and two 105-mm Howitzers. A pillar lists residents and their wartime service, from the Spanish-American War to the Vietnam War. This same pillar describes the war and the dates that these wars were declared and ended. There is also a panel for the Franklin Park American Legion Post 974, which lists the membership of the post since November 2000.

The Hellenic American Veterans Memorial was erected by the American Legion Hellenic Post 343 at Elmwood Cemetery in River Grove on January 1, 2010. It features four main panels, eight small cube blocks, three flagpoles, and a hedge row on either side of the monument, bordering the east and west sides. The four main panels have inscriptions of names of the fallen and members of Hellenic descent who served in the US military. The first panel is inscribed with a helmet and the following words: "Hellenic American Veterans Memorial Hellenic Post 343, In Memory of Hellenes who have served in the United States Armed Forces from WWI to the present." The small cube blocks are inscribed with single-word inspirational inscriptions—Tribute, Warrior, Pride, Unity, Honor, Nobility, Glory, and Bless.

The Hellenic American Veterans Memorial was officially dedicated in a special ceremony by American Legion Hellenic Post 343 and officiated by Metropolitan Iakovos on July 4. The stunning monument, designed by architect Roula Alakiotou, was erected at Elmwood Cemetery in River Grove overlooking the pond. The memorial pays homage to "Hellenes who have fought in the United States Armed Forces from WWI to the present." Names of the individuals who made the ultimate sacrifice are inscribed into the monument, immortalizing their service. Chairman A. Steve Betzelos thanked everyone for their hard work in creating a fitting tribute to Greek American heroes. The new consul general of Greece, Ioanna Efthymiadou, also addressed the crowd. The event culminated with a 21-gun salute and the playing of "Taps."

The Hopedale Area Veterans Memorial is located at the Hopedale Medical Complex in the Peoria area. The memorial was unveiled on Memorial Day, May 29, 2017. It features a nine-foot-tall sculpture surrounded by six large granite stones, which bear the names of living and deceased veterans from all wars. It features Marine pilot Maj. Reid Nannen, a Hopedale native who was killed during a training accident in Nevada in 2014. Former NASA space shuttle commander Scott Altman was among the dedication speakers. "Vietnam veterans really felt like the forgotten generation when they came back. I think we're especially trying now to honor those folks who come back from Iraq, Afghanistan, but also the people who are doing the military jobs across the world, there's a sacrifice that they all make," he said.

The Itasca Veterans Memorial consists of a dedication stone, the US flag, five monuments, and flags representing the various services. The memorial was dedicated in 1995 by the Village of Itasca and cosponsored by VFW Post 5167. The five monuments and flags are prominently featured in the Itasca Veterans Memorial and represent the individual branches of the United States armed forces. Distinguished Service Medals sit below the seals of the branches.

The Douglas County Veterans Memorial is located at the Douglas County Courthouse. It was dedicated on November 11, 2005, by the American Legion and Veterans of Foreign Wars posts and funded entirely with private donations. In recognition of the men and women who served in peace and war, the plaque reads, "As they pass to the sound of distant drums and the muted bugle to their final muster, let us not forget their service and sacrifice to this great nation." In the center of the memorial is an M-16 with fixed bayonet pointing to the ground and boots around the rifle muzzle. On top of the rifle butt is a soldier's helmet. Next is a circular design with small upright blocks of black granite pillars representing all branches of the military. On the small plaza that surrounds the memorial is a gray granite walkway where veterans' names are engraved into individual stones. Equally spaced around the small plaza are black granite benches. It is all surrounded by the flags from the services on the outer perimeter.

The Morrison Veteran's Park and Memorial, located by Grove Hill Cemetery, was completed and dedicated on November 11, 2017. It was dedicated by the City of Morrison and Morrison area businesses and serves to immortalize the sacrifices made by area veterans. The park includes a Howitzer field artillery piece, and tablets inscribed with the names of deceased Morrison-area veterans, along with their date of death, burial place, and the war in which they served. Two granite benches, donated by a couple of Morrison service organizations, provide visitors a spot to sit and reflect. The American flag, POW/MIA flag, and the Illinois flag fly overhead.

The Metamora American Legion Honor Roll Memorial, funded by the Metamora Lions Club, was built in October 1942. The cobblestone memorial was 8 feet high and 16 feet wide. The base and frame for the honor roll surface were constructed of native stones that were gathered by local citizens. The memorial was dedicated to the men and women from Metamora and the surrounding area who served in the United States armed forces.

The Kiwanis Memorial Park, located in Paris, was dedicated on November 8, 1948. The memorial honors veterans who perished in World War I, World War II, the Vietnam War, and the Gulf Wars. A memorial is erected on the park grounds in the center with the inscription: "In Memory of Those Who Gave Their Lives from Edgar County World War I & II. Lest We Forget." It also lists the names of those who died in the wars.

On Memorial Day, May 31, 1999, the Village of Niles dedicated the Veteran's Memorial Waterfall as a monument in memory of those Niles residents who served their country. Since its dedication, a ceremony is held at the site every Memorial Day and Veterans Day in memory of those residents who served in the armed forces. A plaque is inscribed: "As water is essential for life, freedom and liberty are essential for living. Let this waterfall be a constant reminder of the sacrifices made to secure liberty. We honor our veterans for their bravery, dedication and patriotism. The citizens of Niles thank you." On the same day, the Niles VFW Post 7712 included a plaque that had been previously located at its post site. It reads, "Dedicated to all POWs–MIAs and to those who served in the Republic of Vietnam 1961–1975, May 26, 1985."

The Village of River Grove Veterans Memorial is located on the front lawn of the Village Hall. The monuments pay homage to residents who served and, in some cases, died in World War II, Korea, and Vietnam. The World War II Veterans Memorial was erected in 1945. The Korean Veterans Memorial was dedicated on June 19, 1993. The Vietnam Veterans Memorial was dedicated on Memorial Day, May 30, 1988. Flying above are the Illinois bicentennial flag, the US flag, and the River Grove flag.

The Tremont Veterans Memorial was dedicated on November 11, 2011. The Tremont American Legion Post 1236 conducted the dedication ceremony. Taking part in the dedication was the village president, Miss Tremont, Tremont Boy Scouts, the Tremont High School band, and several other community organizations. The memorial features a ship's anchor, a black polished granite monument, two black polished granite benches, two boulders, and memorial bricks leading to the US flag.

The South Holland Veterans Memorial Park was dedicated on Memorial Day, May 26, 2008, by the American Legion Post 883 and the Village of South Holland. It honors all who have served in the armed forces of the United States. The memorial features a brown marble pedestal at center emblazoned with the crests of each branch of the armed forces, topped by an eagle with spread wings, surrounded by slabs of brown marble denoting the various wars and names of residents who served in those wars. The monument recognizes the following wars and the names of current and former South Holland residents who served during both times of conflict and in peace: World War I, World War II, the Korean War, the Vietnam War, Operation Desert Storm, Operation Enduring Freedom, Operation Iraqi Freedom, Panama, Bay of Pigs, Jordan, and Grenada.

The Stockton Veterans Memorial is located in Stockton and was dedicated on July 13, 2015, to all veterans. The mission of the Stockton Veteran's Memorial Committee was to honor all veterans of the Stockton area, living or dead, who have served the military of the United States honorably by commemorating a veteran's memorial in their names. The memorial features a bronze centerpiece eagle perched atop a globe, which sits on top of a granite pedestal that has the insignia of all of the military branches carved into it. Additionally, it has granite walls inscribed with the wars and the names of those who served in those wars, granite benches inscribed with donor or veteran names and images, memorial bricks, and the flags of all the military branches and the US flag.

INDEX